FIRST 15 LESSONS

**Includes Audio
& Video Access**

JAZZ GUITAR

by Joe Charupakorn

T0081896

ISBN 978-1-5400-3796-1

HAL•LEONARD®

Contact us:
Hal Leonard
7777 West Bluemound Road
Milwaukee, WI 53213
Email: info@halleonard.com

In Europe, contact:
Hal Leonard Europe Limited
42 Wigmore Street
Marylebone, London, W1U 2RN
Email: info@halleonardeurope.com

In Australia, contact:
Hal Leonard Australia Pty. Ltd.
4 Lentara Court
Cheltenham, Victoria, 3192 Australia
Email: info@halleonard.com.au

PLAYBACK+
Speed • Pitch • Balance • Loop

To access audio and video visit:
www.halleonard.com/mylibrary
Enter Code
2097-5751-8873-0312

In this book, we're going to get you started on playing jazz guitar. If you already have a solid grasp of guitar basics like barre chords, this book will provide an effortless transition into the world of jazz guitar. If you're a complete beginner, the material in this book is still very manageable, and the included audio and video tracks will be of great help. Before we begin to actually play the guitar, we're going to briefly go over how to get a conventional jazz sound. Let's get started...

DIALING IN A JAZZ SOUND

Nowadays, jazz guitar is played on every guitar type from solidbody guitars like the Telecaster to semi-hollowbody guitars like the Gibson ES-335. But traditionally, the jazz guitar sound consisted of a single-cutaway archtop hollowbody like the Gibson L-5 or ES-175, or the Ibanez GB200, played with heavy-gauge strings like .012–.052. No matter what type of guitar you are playing, you can get a ballpark traditional jazz guitar sound by using the warmer-sounding neck pickup with the tone control rolled off.

Amps like the Fender Twin Reverb, Fender Deluxe Reverb, Roland Jazz Chorus, and Polytone Mini-Brute are some of the most common choices. Effects like overdrive and delay weren't used much, if at all, in straight-ahead jazz. Since the emergence of fusion, these types of sounds have become accepted, and even today, young jazzers playing in a traditional style are not afraid of using effects.

Any of the guitars and amps mentioned above would give you a great foundation to work with. If there are budgetary concerns, you can also look for more affordable lines like Epiphone (owned by Gibson) or Ibanez's Artcore series.

MOVEABLE DOMINANT 7TH CHORDS

Most jazz harmony is based on 7th chords and beyond. That's why jazz has such a colorful sound compared to the simpler, *triad-based* (three-note chords like C, F, and G) harmonic vocabulary of pop, folk, and country music.

The first chord we're going to look at is the *dominant 7th chord* (more commonly referred to as "7th chord" or just "7"), which is simply a major triad with a flat 7th added. For example, in the key of C major (C–D–E–F–G–A–B), the C major triad contains the notes C, E, and G (root–3rd–5th). A C7 chord contains the notes C, E, G, and Bb. The C major scale's 7th note is B, but the C7 chord has a Bb, which is the flatted 7th.

C major scale	C	D	E	F	G	A	B
	1	2	3	4	5	6	7
C7 chord	C		E		G		Bb
	1		3		5		b7

We'll check out two very common and essential 7th chord shapes.

Sixth-String Root

The first moveable chord shape we'll look at is related to this familiar major barre chord. Our example is in C.

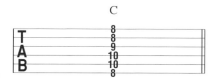

Now, remove your pinky and use the pressure of the barre to catch the note on the D string. This will transform the major barre chord into a 7th chord.

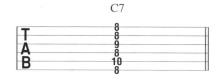

The shape you just learned is *moveable*, meaning you can take the same shape and start it on different frets to get different chords (of the same quality). Because no open strings are involved, we can move these shapes up and down the neck to play them from any root. The chord we looked at is called C7 because the root is on the 6th string, and the note on the 8th fret of the 6th string is C. Regardless of the chord's quality (major, minor, etc.), the chord always gets its name from the root—C is the root for C, Cm, C7, and so on. Here's a chart showing all the note names on the 6th string. Refer to this chart when moving 7th chords with 6th-string roots up and down the neck.

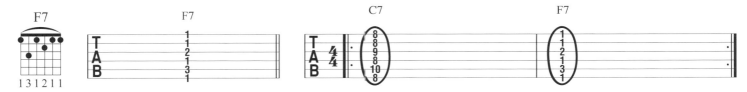

E	F	F#/Gb	G	G#/Ab	A	A#/Bb	B	C	C#/Db	D	D#/Eb	E
0	1	2	3	4	5	6	7	8	9	10	11	12

Let's practice moving the 7th chord shape we just learned. If we move the chord to start on the 1st fret of the 6th string, we get an F7 chord.

Fifth-String Root

Now we'll learn the moveable 7th chord shape with its root on the fifth string. First, play this familiar C major barre chord shape, which starts on the third fret.

Now, replace the middle finger with the ring finger and use the pressure of the barre to catch the note on the G string.

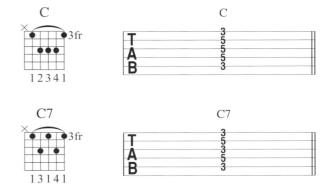

This shape has its root on the fifth string. If you don't already know the names of the notes on the fifth string, here's a chart.

A	A#/Bb	B	C	C#/Db	D	D#/Eb	E	F	F#/Gb	G	G#/Ab	A
0	1	2	3	4	5	6	7	8	9	10	11	12

Practicing and Memorizing the Dominant 7th Chord Shapes

Try to commit to memory the note names on both the fifth and sixth strings. Also, memorize the chord shapes by playing the exact same chords, first with their roots on the sixth string, then with their roots on the fifth string.

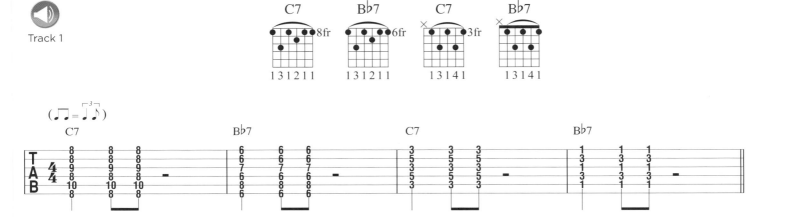

3

BLUES IN C

If you're like most guitarists, you've probably learned how to play the blues somewhere along the way. Jazz music is steeped in the blues tradition, and while the 12-bar structure of jazz blues is similar to that of rock blues, 7th chords and beyond are used, giving it a more colorful sound.

The blues, in its simplest form, consists of three chords—I, IV, and V (more on this in Lesson 11). This means that the I chord has a root that starts on the first note of a given key. In the key of C, the first note is C, and thus, the I chord is also C. Counting alphabetically, the IV chord is F and the V chord is G.

Let's start by playing a blues in C, using only the moveable shape with the sixth-string root. We'll play these three chords in a *four-to-the-bar* style, which uses long strums on beats 1 and 3 and staccato strums on beats 2 and 4 (shown with a dot below the tab numbers). This style of *comping* (playing the chords) is very common in big band music.

Track 2

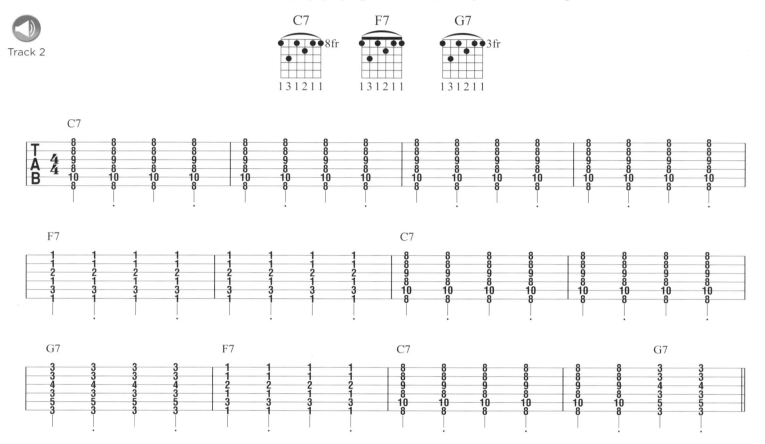

Now, let's play the same blues in C using only the moveable shape with the fifth-string root.

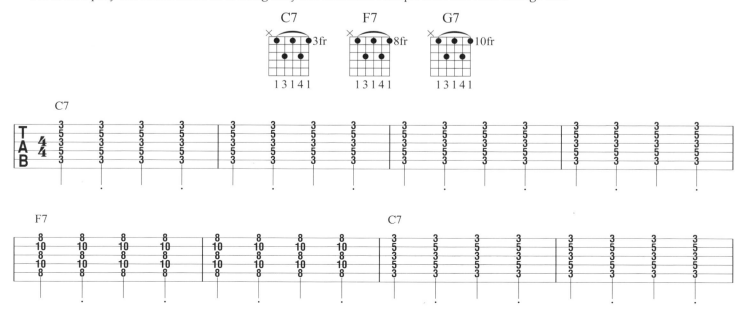

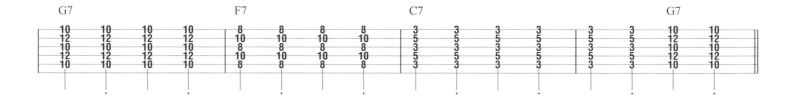

Next, we'll play this progression with both shapes, starting with the sixth-string shape and centering our focus higher up the neck.

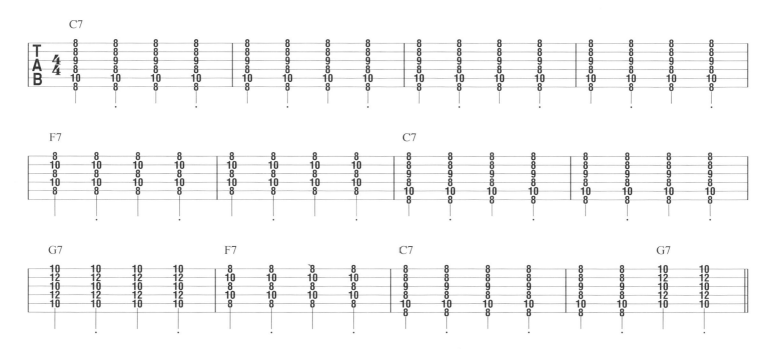

Now, start with a fifth-string shape, which results in playing in a lower area of the neck. This example also features the "Charleston Rhythm" (playing on beat 1 and the "and" of beat 2) and a *quick change*, meaning that in measure 2, you switch to the IV chord and then back to I in measure 3.

Track 3

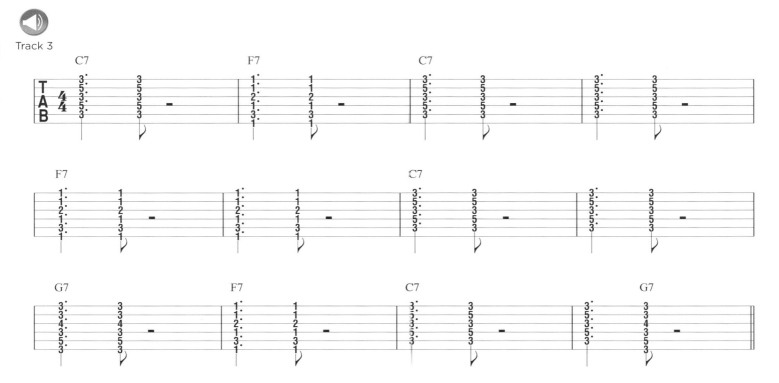

Now that you've got a handle on the blues progression, we're going to take a look at moveable shapes for minor pentatonic and blues scales, which are among the most common scales to use over the blues. This will give us a chance to explore single-note soloing for the first time.

MOVEABLE MINOR PENTATONIC SCALES

Like the 7th chords we learned, these minor pentatonic and blues scale shapes are moveable. First, we'll look at these scales starting with a 6th-string root, since this is the most commonly played shape.

If you are coming from a rock background, you probably know this *minor pentatonic scale* shape. You most likely learned it in A or E, but we're going to look at it in C. Notice in the scale diagrams that the tonics, or root notes, are indicated with white circles.

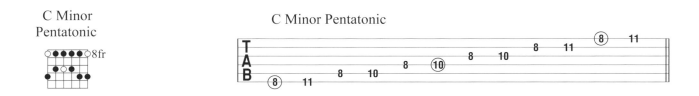

By itself, a scale doesn't sound much like music. It's how you use the notes in a scale that counts. The best way to get a grasp on this is to listen to how the masters like Wes Montgomery, Grant Green, and George Benson use these scales.

In addition to listening, it's also important to develop a vocabulary by learning licks. Now, you don't want to just stick licks into a solo, but having a catalog of licks to draw from will give you phrases that you can manipulate in real time.

MINOR PENTATONIC LICKS

Here are two licks derived from C minor pentatonic. Though jazz guitarists typically avoid bends and vibrato as expressive devices, slides are commonly used; they are included in these licks to add to the bluesy vibe. Play these examples with a *swing rhythm*, in which eighth notes are treated like the first and last notes of an eighth-note triplet, with the middle note left out. In this book, the swing rhythm is indicated by the symbol (♫ = ♩♪).

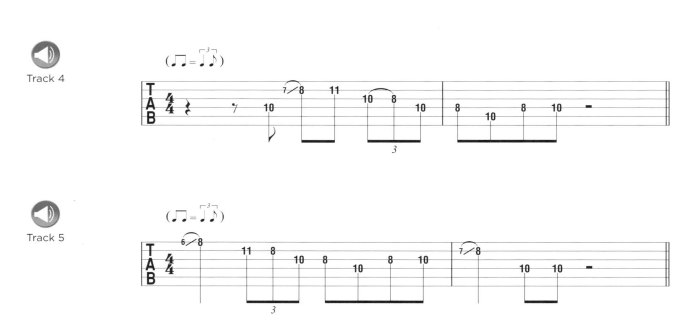

MOVEABLE BLUES SCALES

The *blues scale* is simply a minor pentatonic scale with a ♭5 added. If you compare the C minor pentatonic and blues scale shapes here, there are only two differences: the 9th-fret note on the fifth string and the 11th-fret note on the third string.

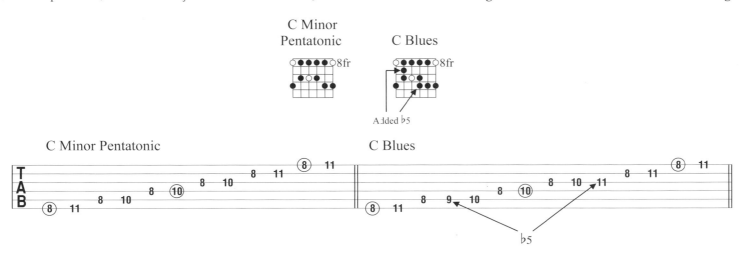

BLUES SCALE LICKS

The ♭5 note of the blues scale adds an extra funky or bluesy sound. Here are some examples of what this sounds like.

Track 6

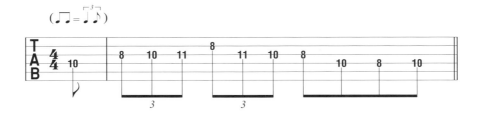

Repetition is a key ingredient in blues phrasing. This lick repeats a six-note fragment three times before coming to a conclusion.

Track 7

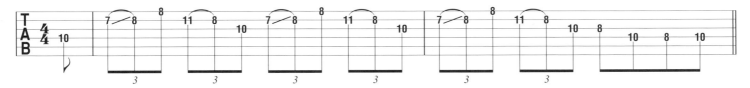

7

LESSON 4

Now that we're familiar with moveable 7th chords, the minor pentatonic scale, and the blues scale, we're going to check out the all-important minor 7th chord. As we did with the dominant 7th chords, we'll focus on two shapes—the ones with sixth- and fifth-string roots.

MOVEABLE MINOR 7TH CHORDS

The *minor 7th chord* is simply a minor triad with a flat 7th added. For example, in the key of C minor (C–D–Eb–F–G–Ab–Bb), the C minor triad contains the notes C, Eb, and G. The C minor 7th chord contains the notes C, Eb, G, and Bb.

Sixth-String Root

In Lesson 1, we made a slight adjustment to a major barre chord to create a dominant 7th chord. In the same way, the minor 7th chord with a 6th-string root is related to its minor barre chord cousin. Here, the difference is that the note on the 4th string is two frets lower and sounded by the barre.

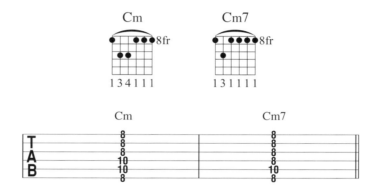

Oftentimes, on this minor 7th chord shape, the fifth and first strings aren't played. The sixth-string note is commonly fretted by the middle finger, with a ring-finger barre covering the fourth through second strings.

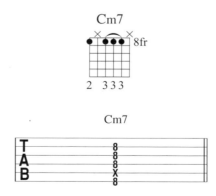

This shape can also be played with a separate finger on each note.

Fifth-String Root

Here's the fingering for the minor 7th chord with a fifth-string root. This shape is similar to the fifth-string root minor barre chord, except here, the note on the third string is two frets lower and fretted by the barre.

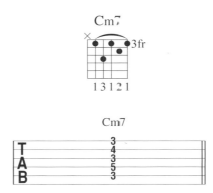

Practicing and Memorizing the Minor 7th Chord Shapes

As we did earlier with dominant 7th chords, let's memorize these chord shapes by playing the exact same minor 7th chords, first with their roots on the fifth string and then with their roots on the fifth string.

Track 8

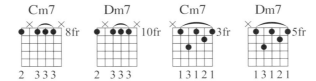

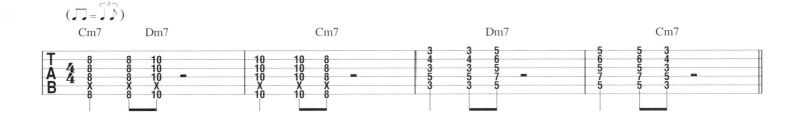

In this lesson, we'll check out the major 7th chord, which is often the tonic chord in jazz songs.

MOVEABLE MAJOR 7TH CHORDS

The *major 7th chord* is simply a major triad with a major 7th added. For example, in the key of C major (C–D–E–F–G–A–B), the C major triad contains the notes C, E, and G. The C major 7th chord contains the notes C, E, G, and B.

Sixth-String Root

The major 7th chord with a sixth-string root is related to its major barre chord cousin. However, in the major 7th chord shape, there's no note played on the fifth string; you'll use the underside of your fretting-hand index finger to mute it, or you can pluck the chord using your thumb on the sixth string and index, middle, and ring fingers on the fourth through second strings, respectively. Also, the note on the fourth string is moved back one fret and the first string is not played at all.

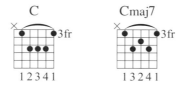

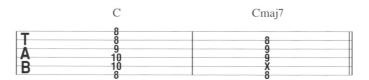

Fifth-String Root

Here's the fingering for the major 7th chord with its root on the fifth string. This shape is similar to the major barre chord with its root on the fifth string, except the note on the third string is moved one fret lower.

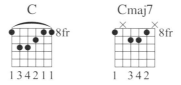

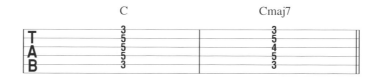

Practicing and Memorizing the Major 7th Chord Shapes

Let's run through some major 7th chords, starting with the shape with the sixth-string root and then moving to the shape with the fifth-string root.

Track 9

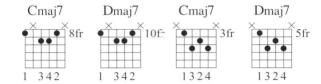

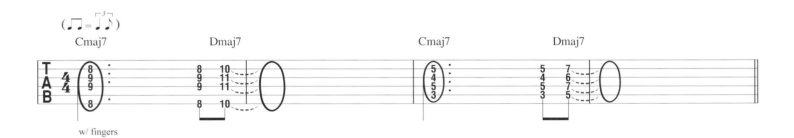

In the first five lessons, we've covered the most common types of 7th chords (7, m7, and maj7). Now, we're going to shift our focus to other essential chords used in jazz.

OTHER COMMON MOVEABLE JAZZ CHORDS
Minor 6th Chord

In minor-key songs, the tonic chord is often played as a *minor 6th chord,* which has a nice, dark quality. Also shown as m6, this chord is a minor triad with a major 6th added, and it is commonly used in Gypsy jazz.

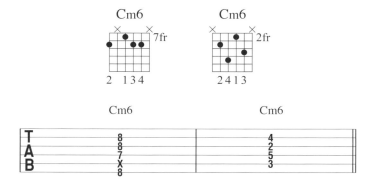

Minor-Major 7th Chord

Another minor-family chord is the *minor-major 7th chord,* which is a minor triad with a major 7th. Also shown as m(maj7), this chord is harmonically rich and is also often used as a tonic chord.

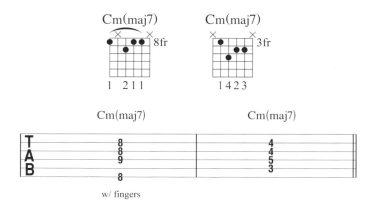

A common movement on minor chords is to have an inner voice descend chromatically from the root to the 6th. The chords generated from this movement are as follows: minor, minor-major 7th, minor 7th, and minor 6th.

You'll hear this move in songs like "My Funny Valentine." If you compare all four chord shapes here, you'll notice that the only differences between them are the notes on the third string. The notes on the other strings are the same throughout the whole chord sequence.

My Funny Valentine

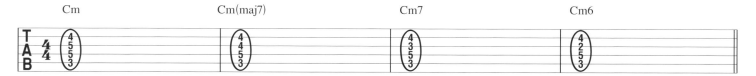

from BABES IN ARMS
Words by Lorenz Hart
Music by Richard Rodgers
Copyright © 1937 WC Music Corp. and Williamson Music Company c/o Concord Music Publishing
Copyright Renewed
All Rights Reserved   Used by Permission

Minor 7th ♭5 Chord

The *minor 7th ♭5* chord can be thought of as a minor 7th chord with its 5th flatted, although it usually isn't used as a direct substitution for a minor 7th chord. Also written as m7♭5, you'll often hear this chord in minor-key tunes or Latin jazz compositions as a iim7♭5 chord that goes to the V and then ultimately to the i chord. These are the two most common fingerings for the m7♭5 chord, with roots on the sixth and fifth strings, respectively.

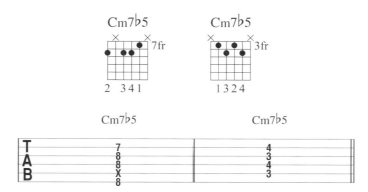

Other than the m7♭5, the minor chords we looked at in this chapter can work as substitutions for a minor 7th chord. For maj7 chords, two very common substitutions are the 6 and 6/9 chords.

6th Chord

The *6th chord* is a major triad with an added major 6th, and it is a common sound in Western swing. It's also used in jazz as a tonic chord, and in long stretches of a major chord (two or more measures), it can alternate with maj7 chords to create movement.

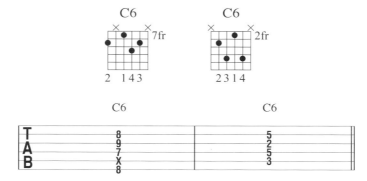

The 6/9 Chord

The *6/9 chord* is used often in bossa novas. While the chord's name sounds fancy, it's actually a very easy chord to finger. In both the sixth- and fifth-string root shapes, an index-finger barre covers the inner strings, the middle finger catches the root, and the ring and pinky fingers cover the upper strings.

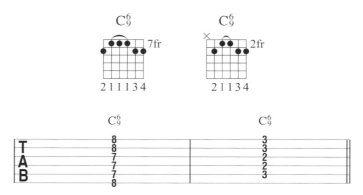

Most times when you see sheet music in jazz, the chords are written in generalities, and you, as the player, are expected to know how to interpret what you see. In this lesson, we're going to look at how to read chord charts.

READING CHORD SYMBOLS

In general, the three most common chord types you'll encounter in jazz are the 7, m7, and maj7. This isn't to say that you won't see other chord types—the m7♭5 chord we checked out in the previous lesson is also used frequently—but these three make up the bulk of the chords you'll see in classic standards.

Depending on where the sheet music is from, you'll see those basic chord types written with various symbols:

- Minor 7th chords might be written as m7, minor 7, -7, or min7.
- Major 7th chords might be written as maj7, Maj7, maj, or Δ7.
- Minor 7th ♭5 chords might be written as m7♭5 or °7.

No matter how the chord symbol is written, it refers to the same thing.

CHORD REDUCTION

Though this book won't cover extended (9th, 11th, and 13th) and altered chords, you might see them written in charts. The good news is that even if you see a complex-looking chord like G13♭9, it will most likely fit into one of the three basic chord types we just discussed—7, m7, and maj7.

The 7 Chord

If a chord has a root and only a number or numbers after it without an "m" or "maj" designation, the chord is dominant, and you can likely just play a 7th chord in its place. For example, if you see C9, C11, or C13, you can often just play a simple C7.

The m7 Chord

If a chord has an "m" after it, you can usually play a m7 chord. For example, if you see chords like Cm6, Cm9, Cm11, Cm13, or Cm6/9, you can usually just play Cm7.

The maj7 Chord

If a chord has "maj" and a number after it, you can usually play a maj7 chord. For example, if you see chords like Cmaj9 or Cmaj13, you can usually just play Cmaj7.

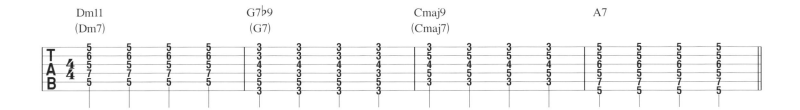

CHORD ENHANCEMENT

The opposite of chord reduction, which we just looked at, is *chord enhancement*. In sheet music, you might see basic labels of three chord types: 7, m7, and maj7. If you know fancier versions of these chords, you can apply direct substitution and replace the simpler chords with the harmonically richer versions. We haven't covered every possible chord type listed here but if you are curious, you can refer to a jazz chord book.

Basic Chord	Direct Substitution
7	9, 11, 13, 7sus4, 7♭5, 7♯5
m7	m6, m6/9, m9, m11, m13
maj7	6, 6/9, maj9, maj13, add9

THE JAZZ BLUES PROGRESSION

When jazz musicians play the blues progression, they'll typically embellish the changes with some ii–Vs ("two–fives"), a topic we'll look at in-depth in Lesson 12. In a nutshell, you'll often see the jazz blues progression as follows:

- Quick change in measure 2
- VI chord in measure 8
- ii chord in measure 9
- V chord in measure 10
- A *turnaround* in the last two measures, which consists of a I–VI–ii–V progression with the chords played for two beats each; the purpose of the turnaround is to set up the beginning of the next *chorus* (or when the chord progression starts over again).

Jazz Blues

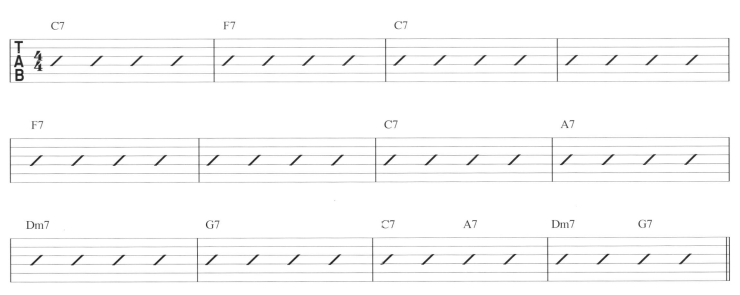

After spending the previous seven lessons learning various chords and scales, it's time to apply them to a full song: Duke Ellington's "C-Jam Blues." This tune is based on the jazz blues progression you just learned. The *head* (or melody) is very easy, and after you get it under your fingers, you should try to memorize it.

Usually in jazz, after playing the head, the band members go around taking solos over the form of the tune. If you have other musicians to play with, practice the song in this order:

1. Play the head.

2. Take a solo over the form of the tune.

3. Comp, or play the chords, for another soloist.

4. Play the head and finish up the tune.

As you get more comfortable, you can also practice *trading 4s*, where each soloist gets four measures of the song's form to solo over, in a round-robin fashion.

C-Jam Blues

Track 10

*Optional on solos.

Now that you know the chords and melody to a jazz classic and are able to play melodies from the minor pentatonic and blues scales, it's time to dig deeper into improvisation. In this lesson, you'll learn some new scales to use over the various chord types we looked at earlier.

MIXOLYDIAN

The dominant 7th chords you worked on have a unique, bluesy sound. That's why minor pentatonic and blues scales work well over them. The funny thing is, in theoretical terms, those scales actually end up giving you "wrong" notes like the ♯9 and ♭5—notes that in, say, a classical music theory class, would be frowned on. But it's this "blues tonality" that gives the blues style its funky character.

Mixolydian is another scale that can be used over dominant 7th chords, and this scale, while still funky sounding, is more directly related to the dominant 7th chord than the minor pentatonic or blues scales. It contains all the 7th chord tones—1, 3, 5, and ♭7—in addition to color tones like the 9th and 13th. (The 11th is also used, though in some cases, it requires special treatment.)

Here are two common Mixolydian fingerings. The first one has its root on the sixth string, and the second one has its root on the fifth string. In the tab, the root notes are circled.

C Mixolydian   C Mixolydian
(sixth-string root) (fifth-string root)

◯ = root

C Mixolydian (sixth-string root)

C Mixolydian (fifth-string root)

Compare the Mixolydian shapes to the C7 chord shapes you learned and note how they overlap. The chord tones are indicated by squares.

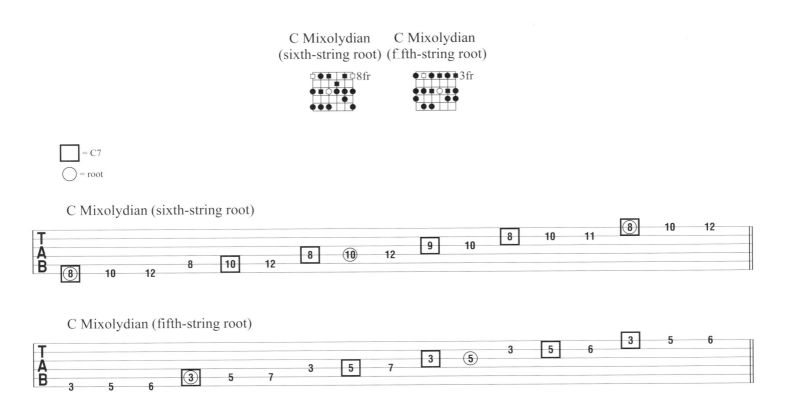

C Mixolydian
(sixth-string root)

C Mixolydian
(fifth-string root)

☐ = C7

◯ = root

C Mixolydian (sixth-string root)

C Mixolydian (fifth-string root)

Let's check out how Mixolydian is used by the masters. In the opening of his solo to the Latin-esque "Cariba," the great Wes Montgomery used B♭ Mixolydian. Check out how he's not just running up and down the scale. Rather, he's using it as a resource to create a musical statement. That approach is how you should use every scale you learn—as a resource in your musical toolbox to draw from.

Cariba

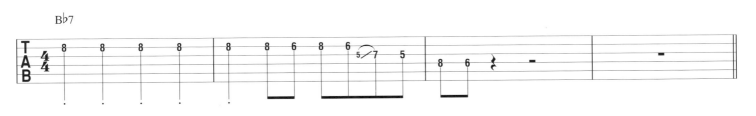

By John L. "Wes" Montgomery
Copyright © 1965 (Renewed) by TAGGIE MUSIC CO., a division of Gopam Enterprises, Inc.
All Rights Reserved

Dorian is another essential scale for jazz improvisers, as well as a signature component of groove-based styles like fusion and funk. In this lesson, we'll take a look at this important tonality.

DORIAN

Dorian is usually the first scale choice jazzers go for when soloing over a minor 7th chord. It contains all of the m7's chord tones—1, ♭3, 5, and ♭7—and also contains the color tones 9, 11, and 13.

Here are two common Dorian fingerings. The first one has a sixth-string root, and the second one has a fifth-string root. Again, the root notes are circled in the tab.

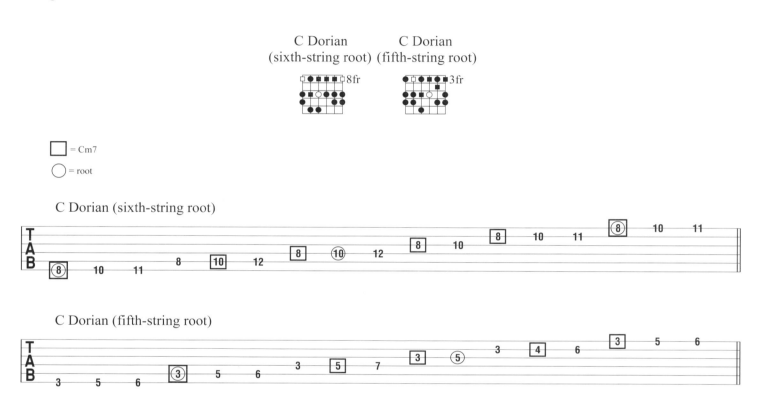

The 13th, in particular, is the note that gives Dorian its signature sound. Listen to it sustained against the Cm7 chord and try to ingrain the sound in your head. If this tonality is new to you, it might sound strange at first, but it's used in pop songs like "Scarborough Fair" and "Eleanor Rigby." It's also the core sound of Santana's "Oye Como Va." Here are a couple of Dorian licks to try.

Track 11

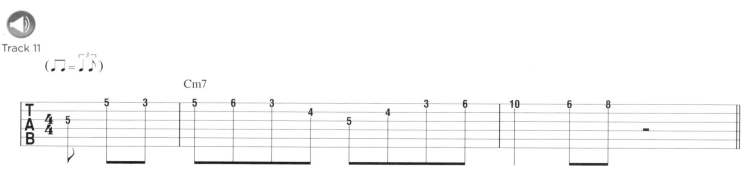

Track 12

DORIAN COMPING

A common comping figure used in the Dorian tonality is a shape based on stacked 4ths. This voicing is a nice substitute for the regular, fifth-string root Cm7 voicing you learned earlier.

That stacked-4ths voicing is also commonly used in conjunction with the same shape played two frets higher.

Miles Davis's *Kind of Blue*, possibly the most influential jazz album of all time, ushered in the modal jazz period. This style featured songs with fewer chord changes and more emphasis on static chords and one-chord vamps—sometimes, only one chord would be used for 16 measures. Here, the two comping shapes we just looked at are employed.

So What

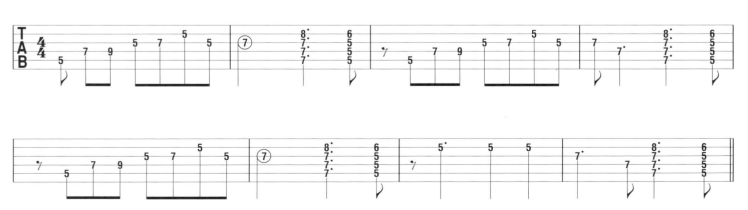

We've explored the funky and jazzy sounds of Mixolydian and Dorian, but it's equally important to look at *Ionian*.

IONIAN

The Ionian mode, also known as the major scale, is as fundamental as it gets. But unlike Mixolydian and Dorian, which are more often seen in jazz and funk styles, Ionian has been used in every genre of music from classical to pop to folk. In jazz, Ionian also gets play time and is among the first choices to use over maj7 chords.

Here are two Ionian fingerings. The first has its root on the sixth string, and the second has its root on the fifth string.

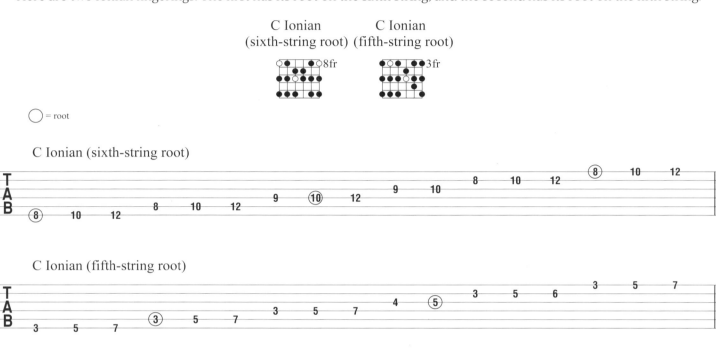

Compare the Ionian shapes to the Cmaj7 chord shapes you learned, and note how they overlap.

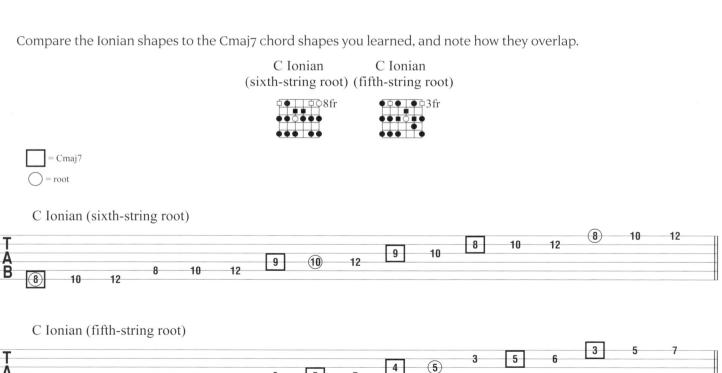

While not as bluesy as Dorian and Mixolydian, Ionian is a great choice for creating catchy melodies. A great example of a straightforward G Ionian melody is in the B section of the jazz standard "A Nightingale Sang in Berkeley Square."

A Nightingale Sang in Berkeley Square

DIATONIC HARMONY

Ionian is also used to draw chord progressions from. Chords can be built from every scale degree of Ionian and are labeled by Roman numerals. We touched briefly on the I, IV, and V chords in Lesson 2, but we'll go into more detail here.

The chords that naturally occur in Ionian are:

Scale Degree	Triad	7th Chord
I	major	major 7th
ii	minor	minor 7th
iii	minor	minor 7th
IV	major	major 7th
V	major	dominant 7th
vi	minor	minor 7th
vii	diminished	minor 7th ♭5

Looking at that chart, you'll note that:

- Major 7th chords naturally occur on the first (I) and fourth (IV) notes of Ionian.
- Minor 7th chords naturally occur on the second (ii), third (iii), and sixth (vi) notes of Ionian.
- A dominant 7th chord naturally occurs on the fifth (V) note of Ionian.
- A minor 7th ♭5 chord naturally occurs on the seventh (vii) note of Ionian.

This formula applies to any Ionian scale; it doesn't matter what key you're in.

CIRCLE OF FIFTHS

The *circle of 5ths* visually represents the order of keys going up in 5ths, and it is useful to know, as many chord progressions move through this cycle. Each successive key has an added sharp. Two adjacent keys contain virtually the same notes with the only difference being the sharped note. The closer two keys are to each other in the circle, the more closely related and consonant they are. The farther away two keys are, the more dissonant the relationship.

Going counterclockwise on the circle, you get the *circle of 4ths*, which represents the order of keys going up in 4ths. Each successive key differs by the addition of a flat.

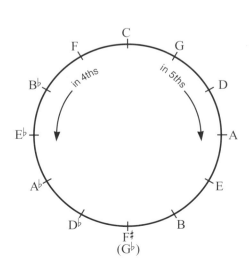

In this lesson, we're going to take a look at the ii–V–I progression, which is unquestionably the most important chord progression in jazz. Virtually all classic jazz standards use this progression or a closely related variation on it, and it's essential that you understand it. To play jazz, you really need to have ii–V–I voicings and phrases under your belt.

THE II–V–I PROGRESSION

The ii–V–I progression consists of a minor 7th chord built on the second note of the major scale, going up to a dominant 7th chord built on the fifth note of the major scale, and resolving to a major 7th chord built on the first note of the major scale. In other cases, like the blues, the I chord would be a dominant 7th chord.

In the key of C, the ii–V–I progression consists of:

ii	V	I
Dm7	G7	Cmaj7

In a blues in C, the ii–V–I progression consists of:

ii	V	I
Dm7	G7	C7

Let's examine some ii–V–I fingerings. Miles Davis' "Tune Up" is a great example of ii–V–I progressions moving through different keys. Play through the tune using the Charleston rhythm that we learned earlier.

Tune Up

Track 13

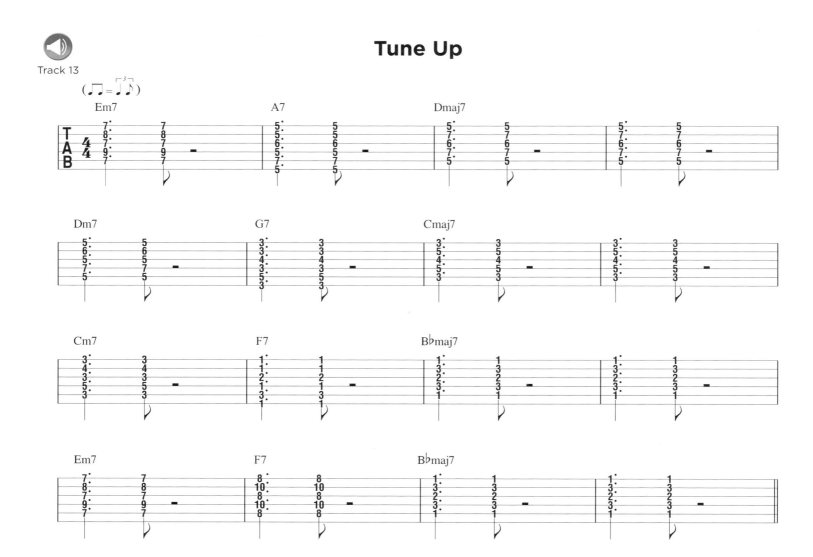

By Miles Davis
Copyright © 1963 Jazz Horn Music Corporation, East St. Louis Music and Second Floor Music
Copyright Renewed
All Rights for Jazz Horn Music Corporation Administered by Downtown DMP Songs
All Rights Reserved   Used by Permission

In addition to internalizing ii–V–I chord shapes, jazz improvisers have a large catalog of ii–V–I patterns at their disposal. Though you don't want to just stick licks over ii–V–Is, having a vast resource to draw from will make it easier to navigate the progression when you come across it.

II–V–I LICKS

Even the melodies of classic jazz songs contain ii–V–I phrases that should be committed to memory. The ii–V–I progressions commonly occur in different harmonic rhythms. Two of the most common are: 1) the ii and V chords lasting one chord per measure, and 2) the ii and V chords each taking up half a measure.

The phrases used over the ii–V–Is in the *head* (melody) to "Groovin' High" are great examples of ii–V–I melodies. Here, the ii and V chords are each one measure long. Here are some other examples to add to your arsenal of ii–V–I phrases.

Groovin' High

When the ii and V chords each last only half a measure (two beats) and the I chord lasts only one measure, the patterns will typically have fewer notes per chord.

Track 14

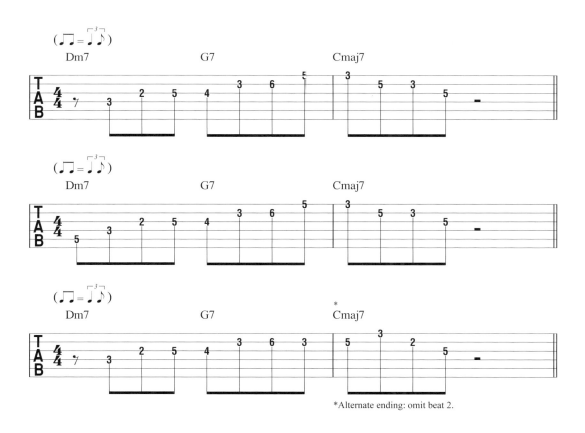

*Alternate ending: omit beat 2.

We've learned a lot of chords, scales, and single-note phrases so far. Now it's time to study rhythm. In jazz, rhythm is very important and gives the music its forward momentum.

COMMON JAZZ RHYTHMS

One of the most distinctive elements of jazz is its rhythmic vitality. The upbeats are often emphasized and syncopation is the norm.

In classical music, you might have a phrase that looks like this:

A jazz interpretation of that rhythm might anticipate the note on beat 3 with an eighth note.

Track 15

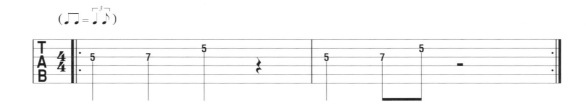

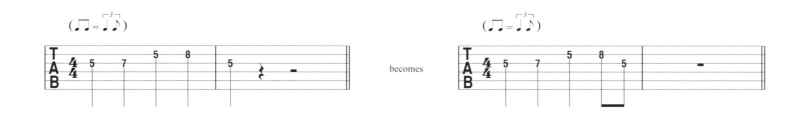

becomes

Rather than always landing squarely on a downbeat, accented and emphasized upbeats are very common. For example, if you check out the melody for the first part of the B section of "Afternoon in Paris," you'll see that the downbeat of each measure is anticipated by an eighth note that occurs on the "and" of beat 4.

Afternoon in Paris

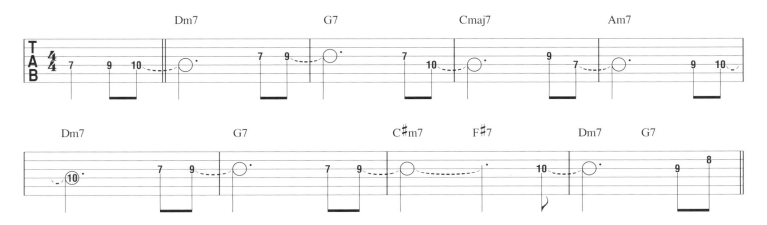

When you practice improvising, rhythm should be at the forefront. Though a lot of faster jazz solos feature long strings of uninterrupted eighth notes, a good solo will also incorporate other rhythmic ideas. In Charlie Parker's "Ornithology," the longer lines are broken up with rhythmic ideas like accented and held upbeat notes.

Ornithology

Arpeggios are the notes of a chord played melodically. Using arpeggios in a solo is a surefire way to outline the underlying chords. They can be played blazingly fast or used melodically, but regardless of how you use them, they are an indispensable tool that every improviser must have.

ARPEGGIO FINGERINGS FOR DOMINANT 7TH, MINOR 7TH, AND MAJOR 7TH CHORDS

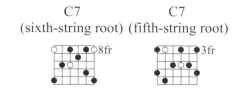

C7
(sixth-string root)

C7
(fifth-string root)

○ = root

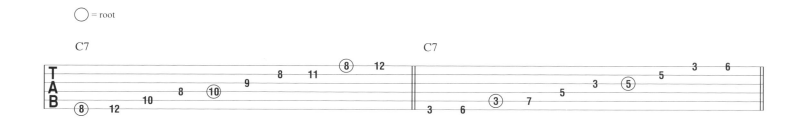

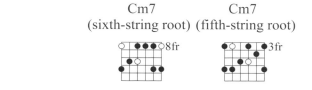

Cm7
(sixth-string root)

Cm7
(fifth-string root)

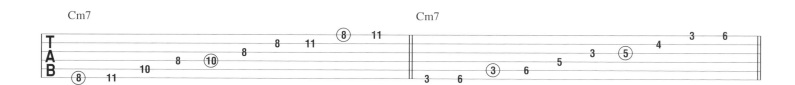

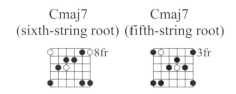

Cmaj7
(sixth-string root)

Cmaj7
(fifth-string root)

 = root

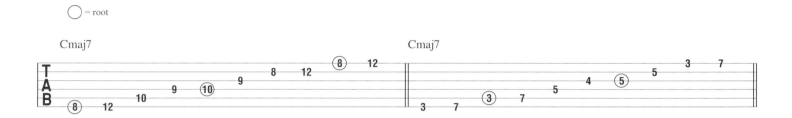

In the first fingering of the Cmaj7 arpeggio above, you can use the seventh fret, fifth string for E in place of the 12th fret, sixth string.

ARPEGGIOS IN ACTION

Just running up and down the arpeggios of a ii–V–I progression, you can clearly hear the chord movement even without any accompaniment.

Track 16

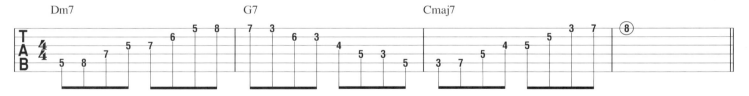

We'll wrap up our studies with the timeless standard "Autumn Leaves." This song uses everything we've looked at—7, m7, and maj7 chords and ii–V–I progressions! After you learn the head and chords, spend time trying to memorize them. Last comes the most fun part, improvising! Take the scales and ii–V–I patterns you've worked on and apply them in your solo, moving them to the appropriate keys. Aim to have a good feel with your eighth notes, staying in time against the accompaniment. You can play over the first three chords thinking A Dorian, D Mixolydian, and G Ionian, or simply play in the key of E minor or G major, since all these chords come from those keys. Note that "Autumn Leaves" is also commonly played in G minor, so after you are comfortable playing it in E minor, try your hand at moving it to G minor. In the performance, I've tagged the last four bars; this is a common way of ending a tune.

Autumn Leaves

Get Better at Guitar

...with these Great Guitar Instruction Books from Hal Leonard!

101 GUITAR TIPS
INCLUDES TAB

STUFF ALL THE PROS KNOW AND USE

by Adam St. James

This book contains invaluable guidance on everything from scales and music theory to truss rod adjustments, proper recording studio set-ups, and much more.

00695737 Book/Online Audio $16.99

AMAZING PHRASING
INCLUDES TAB

by Tom Kolb

This book/audio pack explores all the main components necessary for crafting well-balanced rhythmic and melodic phrases. It also explains how these phrases are put together to form cohesive solos. The companion audio contains 89 demo tracks, most with full-band backing.

00695583 Book/Online Audio $19.99

ARPEGGIOS FOR THE MODERN GUITARIST
INCLUDES TAB

by Tom Kolb

Using this no-nonsense book with online audio, guitarists will learn to apply and execute all types of arpeggio forms using a variety of techniques, including alternate picking, sweep picking, tapping, string skipping, and legato.

00695862 Book/Online Audio $19.99

BLUES YOU CAN USE

by John Ganapes

This comprehensive source for learning blues guitar is designed to develop both your lead and rhythm playing. Includes: 21 complete solos • blues chords, progressions and riffs • turnarounds • movable scales and soloing techniques • string bending • utilizing the entire fingerboard • and more.

00142420 Book/Online Media $19.99

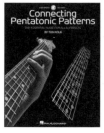

CONNECTING PENTATONIC PATTERNS
INCLUDES TAB

by Tom Kolb

If you've been finding yourself trapped in the pentatonic box, this book is for you! This hands-on book with online audio offers examples for guitar players of all levels, from beginner to advanced. Study this book faithfully, and soon you'll be soloing all over the neck with the greatest of ease.

00696445 Book/Online Audio $19.99

FRETBOARD MASTERY
INCLUDES TAB

by Troy Stetina

Untangle the mysterious regions of the guitar fretboard and unlock your potential. This book familiarizes you with all the shapes you need to know by applying them in real musical examples, thereby reinforcing and reaffirming your newfound knowledge.

00695331 Book/Online Audio $19.99

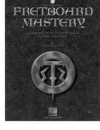

GUITAR AEROBICS
INCLUDES TAB

by Troy Nelson

Here is a daily dose of guitar "vitamins" to keep your chops fine tuned! Musical styles include rock, blues, jazz, metal, country, and funk. Techniques taught include alternate picking, arpeggios, sweep picking, string skipping, legato, string bending, and rhythm guitar.

00695946 Book/Online Audio $19.99

GUITAR CLUES
INCLUDES TAB

OPERATION PENTATONIC

by Greg Koch

Whether you're new to improvising or have been doing it for a while, this book/audio pack will provide loads of delicious licks and tricks that you can use right away, from volume swells and chicken pickin' to intervallic and chordal ideas.

00695827 Book/Online Audio $19.99

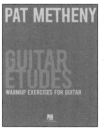

PAT METHENY – GUITAR ETUDES
INCLUDES TAB

Over the years, in many master classes and workshops around the world, Pat has demonstrated the kind of daily workout he puts himself through. This book includes a collection of 14 guitar etudes he created to help you limber up, improve picking technique and build finger independence.

00696587 .... $15.99

PICTURE CHORD ENCYCLOPEDIA

This comprehensive guitar chord resource for all playing styles and levels features five voicings of 44 chord qualities for all twelve keys – 2,640 chords in all! For each, there is a clearly illustrated chord frame, as well as *an actual photo* of the chord being played!.

00695224 .... $19.99

RHYTHM GUITAR 365
INCLUDES TAB

by Troy Nelson

This book provides 365 exercises – one for every day of the year! – to keep your rhythm chops fine tuned. Topics covered include: chord theory; the fundamentals of rhythm; fingerpicking; strum patterns; diatonic and non-diatonic progressions; triads; major and minor keys; and more.

00103627 Book/Online Audio $24.99

SCALE CHORD RELATIONSHIPS
INCLUDES TAB

by Michael Mueller & Jeff Schroedl

This book/audio pack explains how to: recognize keys • analyze chord progressions • use the modes • play over nondiatonic harmony • use harmonic and melodic minor scales • use symmetrical scales • incorporate exotic scales • and much more!

00695563 Book/Online Audio $14.99

SPEED MECHANICS FOR LEAD GUITAR
INCLUDES TAB

by Troy Stetina

Take your playing to the stratosphere with this advanced lead book which will help you develop speed and precision in today's explosive playing styles. Learn the fastest ways to achieve speed and control, secrets to make your practice time really count, and how to open your ears and make your musical ideas more solid and tangible.

00699323 Book/Online Audio $19.99

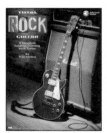

TOTAL ROCK GUITAR
INCLUDES TAB

by Troy Stetina

This comprehensive source for learning rock guitar is designed to develop both lead and rhythm playing. It covers: getting a tone that rocks • open chords, power chords and barre chords • riffs, scales and licks • string bending, strumming, and harmonics • and more.

00695246 Book/Online Audio $19.99

Guitar World Presents STEVE VAI'S GUITAR WORKOUT
INCLUDES TAB

In this book, Steve Vai reveals his path to virtuoso enlightenment with two challenging guitar workouts – one 10-hour and one 30-hour – which include scale and chord exercises, ear training, sight-reading, music theory, and much more.

00119643 .... $14.99

HAL•LEONARD®